TABLE OF CONTENTS

INTRODUCTION

OCTOBER 14, 1908

CUBS SUPREME IN BASEBALL WORLD!

That was a headline in 1908 when the Cubs won the World Series.

In the past century the team's losing ways have become legendary. They have the longest streak of futility in all of professional sports.

There have been a lot of jokes told about the Cubs over the years. A surprising number of people don't take kindly to that and don't appreciate it when their team is the butt of all those jokes. There are now and always have been numerous fans rooting for the Cubs. They have become known as die-hard Cub fans. Their favorite phrase is 'wait 'til next year'.

These people aren't just from Chicago either. They are nationwide and becoming world-wide thanks to being televised on superstation WGN for more than half a century. Watch a Cub game in nearly any city and you'll see blue all throughout the stands. Not just people wearing Cubs Blue but many of them holding signs rooting for them.

I admit I'm a die-hard fan myself. I sometimes listen to their games on the radio while at work. After work I go right to the car and listen some more. When I was young I used to run home from school so I could turn on the TV and see the last innings of the game.

To me there is little in life better than taking my son or daughter to Wrigley Field to take in a game. Going from the hustle and bustle of the city and through the gates is a fantastic experience. From crowded streets and pollution to a paradise of green grass and ivy. A giant scoreboard that has been virtually untouched since 1937. You can see it on old fuzzy highlights that are sometimes shown. For the next several hours at the game life is good.

So why are we Cubs fans like that? There are experts who have theories but I think the main reason is that it's just plain fun. We're eternal optimists. Deep down we know what will happen at the end of the year. The same thing that's happened for a century but who cares? We still cheer and always will.

I take my children to games. My father took me to games. His father took him to games. It's a great way for a father to bond with his children. Enjoyable too.

That's not the point of this book however. The intention here is to take readers back to a time when the fans cheered for the Cubs because they were good. Very good. There was no television or radio broadcasting the games to mass markets like there is today. The fans went to the games just for baseball. And who knows, maybe my great grandfather took my grandfather to games back then.

So let's take a look back one hundred years ago to a time when life was much different than we know it to be now. Not just because the Cubs were a winning team either. I hope you enjoy the journey and find it not just enjoyable but informative too.

1

THE TIMES

The streets then were nothing like they are today. Cars, although beginning to become popular, were still the exception and not the rule. Estimates based on the population and the number of cars built say that there was a maximum possibility of one car per every four hundred forty five people. The reality was less than that due to how many of the originally manufactured cars were no longer on the streets due to accidents, replacement or popularity etc. Horse drawn carriages were not an uncommon form of transportation. Particularly necessary due to the fact there were not yet trucks to deliver necessities to businesses. Electric streetcars were the most common mode of street transportation in Chicago. The first elevated railway – the one that eventually created the Chicago Loop due to how it traveled through downtown – had begun operating in 1891. The Ford Model A began production five years earlier, in 1903. The Model T, the first mass-produced car, was to be introduced in September. And of course passenger airplane travel would not begin for years. The 1920's saw the first small examples of that.

The president of the United States at the time was Theodore Roosevelt. He was the 26th president, taking over from William McKinley in 1901 after his assassination. He would lose the election later that year to William Howard Taft, who got the Republican nomination after Roosevelt declared his candidacy too late. Roosevelt formed the

Progressive party then so he could still run but was beaten. There have been 17 presidents since then.

Women could not yet vote. The 19th amendment that gave them that right would not be passed until 1920. There was no prohibition yet either. That began in 1919 with the 18th amendment and the gangster period began with the illegal sale of alcohol. The United States entered World War I nine years later in 1917. Wrigley Field, old and quaint now, would be built in 1914 and be known then as Weegham Park. The Cubs would begin play there in 1916. In 1920 it would be named Cubs Park, not becoming Wrigley Field until 1926. In 1908 the Cubs played at the West Side Grounds.

In 1908 the Cubs already had an interesting history. They began as the Chicago White Stockings in 1870. In 1871 the Chicago Fire destroyed their stadium – The Union Base-Ball Grounds. They didn't play again until 1874 and the 23rd Street Grounds became their new home. Their name became the Anson Colts, named after Cap Anson, their best player. Finally in 1903 they became the Cubs. That was also the year that the famous double play combination of Tinker, Evers and Chance debuted. Joe Tinker was the shortstop, Johnny Evers the second baseman and Frank Chance handled first base. A poem was written by New York newspaper writer Franklin Pierce Adams about them called *Baseball's Sad Lexicon*. This will be talked about later in this book.

Their manager in 1908 was first baseman Frank Chance. They were the reigning world champions, having beaten the Detroit Tigers in five games in the 1907 World

Series. One of those games was cancelled on account of darkness and declared a tie so Detroit didn't actually win any of the games. From 1905 – 1910 they appeared in four World Series, winning two of them. Their 116 regular season wins in 1906 is still a record today. They won the National League pennant in 1908 with a record of 99-55, finishing one game ahead of the Giants and Pirates, and it was on to the World Series.

2
THE PARK

THE WEST SIDE GROUNDS

The West Side Grounds was also known as West Side Park. The Cubs played there from 1893 to 1915, with 1893 being part time. They played with the White Sox in 1892 at their home field of South Side Park while awaiting the opening of the West Side Grounds. They played there only on Sundays upon it's opening in 1893 and played there exclusively beginning in 1894. They were known as the Anson Colts then. The park's capacity was 16,000. Left field and right field were 340 feet deep whereas center field was a very deep 560 feet. Deepest center field in Wrigley today is 400 feet in comparison. The deepest center field in a ballpark today is Minute Maid Park in Houston at 435 feet.

The West Side Grounds was a wooden structure and Chicago's first park with an upper deck. It was a small upper deck however, going from first base around home plate to third base.

It's biggest claim to fame was a fire that occurred in 1894 on August 5th. It is said that the fire was started by a fan when he threw his lit cigar in the garbage. More than forty fans were injured but there were no fatalities. They were spared when Colts players Walt Wilmot and Jimmy Ryan smashed open a barbed wire fence which was there to keep the fans off the field of play. Fortunately for the fans the breaking of the fence allowed them onto the field and away from the fire to their safety. This incident did not stop the Colts from playing there for any length of time as play continued as normal the next day while the damaged stands were rebuilt. Similar to Wrigley Field today fans were able to see the games from their rooftops behind the outfield.

There were additions to the park as time went on to provide more seating. More box seats were built over the grandstands in back of home plate as well as above the outfield bleachers. The rest of the park was lacking in basic upkeep and the Cubs moved out after the 1915 season. This move would be a permanent one as they began play in 1916 in Weegham Park, named after their owner at the time, Charles Weegham. It would be named Cubs Park in 1920 and finally become known as Wrigley Field in 1926. Wrigley Field was named after team owner William Wrigley Jr., who founded the Wrigley chewing gum company in 1891.

The West Side Grounds remained for a few years after the Cubs left, hosting various events in an effort to still make money, one of them being Buffalo Bill's Wild West Show, but it's poor condition and lack of business led to it being torn down in 1920.

The West Side Grounds

3
THE DEADBALL ERA

Early 20th century baseball went through a time called the deadball era. It is generally agreed upon that it went from 1900-1919. Games at that time were typically low scoring affairs. There are several reason for this which aren't always agreed on by historians A few reasons are universally agreed on however.

One contributing factor to this is the style of baseball that was played during that period. Rather than swinging for the fences there was a lot of offensive strategy involved. Strategies such as stolen bases, hit and runs and bunts were common ways of trying to score runs. This style of play put more emphasis on trying to move runners along the bases, often giving up outs to do so. Sacrifice bunting was common also. The strategy of trying to push one run across discouraged batters from swinging overly hard in an effort to score runs just with hitting.

Playing talented defensive players sometimes detracted from offensive firepower also as this type of player was not necessarily the best hitter at that position.

The making of the ball itself was a contributing factor too. Hence the name deadball. Until 1920 the balls were made by hand, sometimes resulting in slightly looser yarn wrapped around the core of the ball. The wrapping of the yarn around the core took place by machine beginning around 1920, whereby it was likely wound tighter.

Pitches were different too. Spitballs were legal. Scuffing of the ball was legal. These things made the ball move and break more sharply. Those pitches were made illegal in 1920.

One ball was used for the entire game when possible. Foul balls hit in the stands were returned so they could still be used. As games went on the ball became softer from the abuse received from being hit so often. Spit and tobacco juice accumulated on the ball during games, darkening the ball and making it harder to see when batting.

Another factor in the dead ball era was a rule that took effect in 1901 concerning foul balls. Pre-1901 a foul ball was not considered a strike except when bunting. A batter could foul off as many balls as he wanted with no penalty. The adoption of the rule in 1901 that made foul balls strikes changed the style of hitting players had become accustomed to, lowering scores also.

The changing of many of these rules in 1920 helped usher out the dead ball era. There was another contributing factor however. Babe Ruth. His swinging for the fences and prolific number of home runs changed the way many people batted. Bunts were less common and the swing became more of an uppercut as other hitters emulated his style.

More than one ball began being used in games. A rule was enacted that balls were to be removed from the game and replaced by new balls when they became dark and soft. Even the ballparks began changing. The spacious fields that had been played in were changed to smaller hitter friendly ones. It no longer took such a prodigious shot to clear the walls.

Things were more difficult for hitters back then. They faced superstar pitchers such as Christy Mathewson, Walter Johnson and Cy Young to name a few. In the 1920's they were being replaced by superstar hitters like Babe Ruth and Lou Gehrig.

The 1908 Cubs played in the dead ball era. Baseball by all means was still a game of skill. Just different.

4

THE ROSTER

In 1908 the Cubs had a total of 26 players on their roster.

Position Players

Johnny Kling – C, OF
Pat Moran - C
Doc Marshall - C
Frank Chance – 1B
Johnny Evers – 2B, OF
Heinie Zimmerman – 2B, 3B, SS, OF
Harry Steinfeldt – 3B
Sollie Hofman – 1B, 2B, 3B, OF
Johnny Tinker - SS
Jimmy Sheckard - OF
Frank Schulte - OF
Jimmy Slagle - OF
Del Howard – 1B
Kid Durbin - OF
Jack Hayden - OF
Vin Campbell – OF (1 game)

Pitchers

Mordecai Brown - SP
Ed Reulbach - SP
Jack Pfeister - SP
Orval Overall - SP
Chick Fraser - SP
Carl Lundgren - SP

Andy Coakley - RP
Rube Kroh - RP
Carl Spongberg - RP
Bill Mack – RP

5
THE PLAYERS

Johnny Kling
Catcher
Born: February 25, 1875
Died: January 31, 1947

Johnny Kling was the starting catcher for 117 games in 1908, appearing in a total of 126 games. He joined the team in September 1900 and played for them until June 1911. They traded him and three other players in June 1911 to the Boston Rustlers, who were named the Braves at the  beginning of the 1912 season. At the beginning of the 1913 season the Braves traded him to the Cincinnati Reds for a utility player named Tex McDonald and he retired from baseball after the 1913 season. He was the player-manager of the Braves for the 1912 season but they had a dismal record of 52-101. That was his only opportunity to manage.

He was a part-time player until 1902. He became the Cubs' full-time catcher in 1902 when Frank Chance moved from catcher to first base. Despite his offensive talents Chance proved to be poor defensively at catcher but he thrived playing first.

Although he was a more than adequate hitter (he had the second highest batting average on the team in 1908 at .276) it was his defense he was most known for. In the 1907 World Series he threw out 50% of Tiger runners trying to steal a base. The Tigers Ty Cobb, who led the league that year with 49 stolen bases, didn't have one the entire series.

His other talent caused him to miss the 1909 season with the Cubs. He won the World Pocket Billiard Championship in the winter of 1908 and spent 1909 defending his crown. Upon his return to the team in 1910 he was fined $700 by major league baseball but became a full-time player once again.

Twenty years after leaving baseball he bought the Kansas City Blues of the American Association, a minor league team. The Blues were his hometown team. He was the first team owner to desegregate his team's home stadium, allowing people of all races and colors to sit together at the games.

He had one controversy both during and after his baseball career. It concerned his ethnicity. He was considered by some to be Jewish, which would make him the first Jewish baseball player. Others say he was not Jewish but his wife was. Anti-Semitism was rampant in the world in those days and there is a school of thought that this prevented him from being elected to the Hall Of Fame.

FACT

Johnny Kling finished tenth in the league in home runs in 1908 with 4. The low total for a league leader was because of the dead ball.

STATISTICS

OFFENSE

Career

Games	1,260
Batting Avg	.271
Hits	1,151
Home Runs	20
RBI	513

1908

Games	126
Batting Avg	.276
Hits	117
Home Runs	4
RBI	59

DEFENSE

Career

Games	1,260
Fielding %	.970
Errors	217

1908

Games	126
Fielding %	.979
Errors	16

Frank Chance
First Base
Born: September 9, 1876
Died: October 15, 1924

Frank Chance played on the Cubs from 1898–1912, retiring in April 1914. He was a catcher until 1902 when he became the Cubs first baseman, opening up the catcher position for Johnny Kling. He was named manager of the team in 1905, being player-manager of the team until the end of the 1912 season. He retired as a player but managed the  New York Yankees for two seasons, through 1914.

With Frank Chance as manager they won the National League pennant four times, winning the World Series two of those times. His managerial record for the Cubs was 530-235. His nickname was 'Peerless Leader'. It was with him as manager that they played the one and only Chicago subway series against the White Sox in 1906. His team set a record with 116 wins that year, a record which still stands today even though the Seattle Mariners tied the record in 2001. They achieved their tie of the record in the 161st game of a 162 game season however compared to the 154 season in 1906. The Cubs did not win the World Series that year. The White Sox did.

Something Chance is well remembered for is his inclusion in the poem 'Baseball's Sad Lexicon', written by a New York newspaper columnist named Franklin Pierce Adams. The poem is about the Cubs double play combination of Joe Tinker, Johnny Evers and Frank Chance. Tinker to Evers to Chance. The three started playing as a unit in 1902 and stayed together for eight years through the 1910 season.

Chance was well known at the time for his temperament and aggressive style of play. Many of his players were intimidated by him and he used that to both motivate them and keep them in line, doing what he wanted them to do. He got into a fight that year with Heinie Zimmerman, a little-used left fielder on the 1908 team. Victoriously of course.

Others sometimes felt his wrath too. In July of 1907 when Brooklyn Dodger fans were throwing garbage and bottles at him he angrily threw a bottle into the stands in retaliation. A young boy was hit and cut on the leg. The fans rushed the field after the Giants lost 5–0 and Chance had to be taken away to prevent further troubles, being driven home in an armored car for his safety.

His aggressive play was not uncommon at the time. Sliding into second base with spikes in the air to prevent a double play and pitchers intentionally throwing at batters was common.

He stood very close to home plate when batting and had no qualms about reaching base by being hit by a pitch, something else that was not uncommon then. In some cases it still isn't uncommon. He never led the league in being hit by pitches but he was hit a total of 137 times in his fourteen year career. Toward the end of his career he was nearly deaf from the blows to his head. He had surgery to remove a blood clot from his brain in September of 1912. In a double-header on May 30, 1904 against the Cincinnati Reds he set a record by being hit five times. This was in the pre-batting helmet days.

His last two years in the major leagues were spent as player-manager of the New York Yankees. He remained their manager for two years after his playing days but those years were somewhat unsuccessful and they fired him after the 1914 season. His last appearance in baseball was as manager of the Boston Red Sox in 1923. Health problems cut his life short after that year, dying one year later of tuberculosis. His last day on earth was October 15th, 1924. He was 47 years old.

FACT

After the Cubs won the playoff game with the Giants on October eighth Chance was injured by a fan when trying to leave the Polo Grounds. He was struck in the throat when a fan threw an empty bottle at him, injuring cartilage and damaging his vocal cords. He could only whisper. He did not miss any time in the World Series however.

STATISTICS

OFFENSE

Career

Games	1,287
Batting Avg	.296
Hits	1,283
Home Runs	20
RBI	596

1908

Games	129
Batting Avg	.272
Hits	123
Home Runs	2
RBI	55

DEFENSE

Career

Games	997 1B	186 C
Fielding %	.987 1B	.952 C
Errors	135 1B	38 C

1908

Games	126 1B
Fielding %	.979 1B
Errors	15 1B

MANAGER

Career

Games	1,620
Wins	946
Losses	648
Winning %	.593

1908

Games	158
Wins	99
Losses	58
Winning %	.643

Johnny Evers
Second Base
Born: July 21, 1881
Died: March 28, 1947

Johnny Evers was the second baseman on the 1908 Cubs. He began with the Cubs in September 1902 and was initially their shortstop. He switched to second base in 1904 when Frank Chance moved from catcher to first base and Joe Tinker moved from third base to shortstop. This created the famous double play combination immortalized in *'Baseball's Sad Lexicon'*. He played with the Cubs through the 1913 season. Evers was traded to the Boston Braves after 1913, playing with them until the middle of the 1917 season, finishing off that year with the Philadelphia Phillies before retiring.

When Frank Chance left the Cubs after the 1912 season Evers was named player-manager for the 1913 season. He managed just that year during his playing days but did return to manage the Cubs in 1921 and the White Sox in 1924.

He made two final appearances after his retirement. He had one at bat for the White Sox in 1922 and played one inning with one at bat for the Braves in 1929. He made an error in his one inning in the field on his only play.

When World War 1 broke out he went with the Knights Of Columbus to Europe as part of their mission to help the American troops. The Knights visited, provided aid, set up small areas where the troops could stop briefly to write letter home or relax for a bit, and passed out things like gum, cigarettes, baseballs, footballs and boxing gloves. There were even some baseball fields and boxing rings set up for the troops.

In 1908 he was involved in the one play that had the greatest impact on their season. It became known as the 'Merkle Boner'. The game was played on September 23 against the New York Giants. It was the bottom of the ninth inning with the game tied 1-1. With two outs the Giants had Moose McCormick on third, Fred Merkle on first and Al Bridwell batting. Bridwell hit a single driving in McCormick for the run that would give the Giants a 2-1 victory.

On seeing McCormick score the winning run, Fred Merkle, rather than going to second base, started running to the Giant clubhouse in center field. Johnny Evers saw this and called for the ball to step on second, forcing Merkle out as he never touched the base. The ball never got there, though, as it was thrown into the crowd in celebration. After much controversy Merkle was called out at second for the third out of the inning, negating the run scored by McCormick. The game remained tied 1-1 after nine full innings.

There was such a riot in the stadium after the play that the game could not be restarted and was called a tie. It was replayed on October 8 and the Cubs won 4-2. That win gave the Cubs the pennant as the teams were tied with 98 wins apiece, causing it to be considered a one game playoff. The Giants and Pirates were tied for second place, 1 game behind. It can se said that Johnny Evers was the main force behind the Cubs getting to the World Series that year.

The Cubs won game five of the Series 2-0, giving them the championship. In that game Johnny Evers was involved in both runs scored. He scored the first run in the top of inning number one and drove in the second run in the top of the fifth.

In 1914, his first season with the Braves, they won the World Series in a four game sweep of the Philadelphia Athletics, making Evers a three time Series winner in five appearances. The two losses were in 1906 and 1910 with the Cubs.

He was the National League MVP in 1914, three years before he retired.

Johnny Evers died of a cerebral hemorrhage in 1947 at sixty five. Unlike Chance, he lived to see his induction into the Hall Of Fame a year earlier.

FACTS

Johnny Evers was a very small person. One of the smallest in baseball history. He was average in height at 5'9" but he never weighed more than 130 lbs in his playing days.

In 1902, his first year with the Cubs, he weighed just under 100 lbs.

Johnny Evers last name was actually pronounced with a long E at the beginning. Eevers. Although that is how he and his family always pronounced it he never corrected people when they said otherwise, and that is how his name is remembered in history.

Johnny Evers and Joe Tinker got into a fight in late 1905 and didn't speak to each other for more than 30 years. This did not affect their on-field play though as they were always part of an excellent double play combination.

STATISTICS

OFFENSE

Career

Games	1,783
Batting Avg	.270
Hits	1,658
Home Runs	12
RBI	538

1908

Games	126
Batting Avg	.300
Hits	125
Home Runs	0
RBI	37

DEFENSE

Career

Games	1,776
Fielding %	.953
Errors	447

1908

Games	122
Fielding %	.960
Errors	25

Joe Tinker
Shortstop
Born: July 27, 1880
Died: July 27, 1948

Joe Tinker was the shortstop on the 1908 Chicago Cubs, part of the famous Tinker to Evers to Chance double play combination. His first year on the Cubs was 1902, playing with them until being traded to the Reds after the 1912 season. He  played for the Reds for one year. An excellent fielder and an important part of their double play combination, he was a competent hitter and very fast runner, stealing a total of 336 bases in his 11 year career. He had a career batting average of .262 to go with those stolen bases.

In 1908 he led the Cubs in several offensive categories: 146 hits, 6 home runs and 68 RBI. His feud with Johnny Evers that began in 1905 lasted 33 years and ended after the two were both hired to broadcast the Cubs/Yankees World Series in 1938.

Joe Tinker had diabetes and died in 1948 of complications from the disease He did witness his induction to the Hall Of Fame in 1946 when the trio of Tinker, Evers and Chance were elected together.

FACT

On July 17, with the Cubs and Giants tied for the lead, Joe Tinker homered in the seventh inning for the Cubs only run putting them alone in first.

The pitcher he hit best against was the Giants great Christy Mathewson with a .291 career average.

STATISTICS

OFFENSE

Career

Games	1,804
Batting Avg	.262
Hits	1,687
Home Runs	31
RBI	782

1908

Games	157
Batting Avg	.266
Hits	146
Home Runs	6
RBI	68

DEFENSE

Career

Games	1,792
Fielding %	.938
Errors	648

1908

Games	157
Fielding %	.958
Errors	39

Harry Steinfeldt
Third Base
Born: September 29, 1877
Died: August 17, 1914

Harry Steinfeldt was a third baseman on three different teams. Most notably for the Cubs from 1906-1910 during which they appeared in the World Series four times. 1908 was the most famous as it was the team's last championship of the century.

He began his career on the Cincinnati Reds in 1898, playing for them until he was traded to the Cubs after the 1905 season. He played for the Cubs throughout their championship years and finished on the Boston Braves in 1911. He played only a portion of the 1911 season with the Braves as he became ill and suffered a nervous breakdown at the beginning of the 1911 season. He died three years later, in August 1914. The exact cause of his death is not known but is listed as a cerebral hemorrhage on his death certificate.

He didn't start out his life wanting to be a baseball player. He started out as an actor traveling the country in minstrel shows. The story goes that he realized his baseball talents when performing in a baseball game as part of a show that he and his theater group were staging.

His biggest strength was hiw defense, not his offense, although he held his own quite well. In 1926 he hit .327 with a league leading 83 RBI's and 176 hits while also stealing 29 bases. He was high on the team in the 1907 World Series with a batting average of .471 when they swept the Tigers. He led the league in fielding percentage three times on the Cubs, the first time in 1906, the year of his best offensive performance

Due to his untimely death in 1914 he never had an opportunity to manage in the league as some of his teammates on the Cubs did. He died of a cerebral hemorrhage He was just 36 when he died.

FACT

He was the only Cub infielder not mentioned in 'Baseball's Sad Lexicon' because of the position he played, even though he was a vital part of that successful infield.

STATISTICS

OFFENSE

Career

Games	1,646
Batting Avg	.267
Hits	1,576
Home Runs	27
RBI	762

1908

Games	150
Batting Avg	.241
Hits	130
Home Runs	1
RBI	62

DEFENSE

Career

Games	1,642
Fielding %	.927
Errors	463

1908

Games	150
Fielding %	.940
Errors	28

Jimmy Sheckard
Left Field
Born: November 23, 1878
Died: January 15, 1947

Jimmy Sheckard was a much-traveled ballplayer from the late 1800's through the early 1900's. He started in 1897 at age 18 with the Brooklyn Bridegrooms (later the Superbas and eventually the Dodgers), who he came  back to play for two more times during his career. After playing for them through the 1898 season he made a stop in Baltimore, playing for the Baltimore Orioles for a year. He would return to them later also. Then it was back to Brooklyn for two years, the Orioles for another year and Brooklyn for two more before finally landing with the Cubs in 1906, staying there until 1912. They were his one and only steady baseball home.

His best years were in the beginning but he was an effective outfielder and leadoff hitter while with the Cubs. Of course, true to his traveling ways, he spent one last year – 1913 – splitting time with both the St. Louis Cardinals and Cincinnati Reds before retiring from baseball.

The Cubs acquired Sheckard from the Brooklyn Superbas after the 1905 season. His first year on the team, 1906, he batted .262 and played a very good left field. It was the first World Series he appeared in. He went hitless in the Series, not contributing offensively but did not bear sole responsibility for the loss. It is a team sport after all.

He did play for the Cubs for all of their World Series appearances that decade under manager Frank Chance, making him a two-time baseball champion. While credit or blame never rests with one person in baseball, it was a terrific run. He held down an important position on a championship team so he does share some credit for their championship run.

As his production began to erode in his final years with the team they decided to sell him to the Cardinals in 1913 but his baseball playing days were ending. After short stints with the Cardinals and Reds that year he called it quits.

The rest of his life was not so successful. He held some jobs trying to make ends meet after the Stock Market crash of 1929 when he lost most everything. He was hit by a car at 68 while working one of those jobs – at a service station – dying shortly afterwards.

Jimmy Sheckard had several offensive highlights during his career. He led the league in stolen bases two times. Both times before he became a Cub. The first time was with the Brooklyn Superbas in 1899, then again with the Superbas in 1903. 1903 was also the year he had the most home runs in the league with nine. He was talented at knowing the strike zone. He drew many walks during his career, giving him a high on-base percentage and many opportunities to score runs. He led the league in walks in both 1911 and 1912. Not coincidentally, 1911 was the year he led the league in runs scored. This ability helped him get the number of steals he did and made him an excellent leadoff hitter.

FACT

Before the 1906 World Series against the Hitless Wonder White Sox he told people he would easily bat .400 against them. Instead he went 0 for 21 as the Cubs lost the Series in six games.

STATISTICS

OFFENSE

Career

Games	2,122
Batting Avg	.274
Hits	2,084
Home Runs	56
RBI	813

1908

Games	115
Batting Avg	.231
Hits	93
Home Runs	2
RBI	22

DEFENSE

Career

Games	2,098
Fielding %	.953
Errors	230

1908

Games	115
Fielding %	.955
Errors	10

Jimmy Slagle
Center Field
Born: July 11, 1873
Died: May 10, 1956

Jimmy Slagle played for ten years in the major leagues on four teams. He played for three of those teams before settling on the Cubs in 1902 and played the rest of his career there, retiring after the 1908 season. He did  not play in the 1908 World Series, being replaced in center field by Solly Hofman, who had been a utility man up until then, playing all four infield positions and all three outfield positions.

Slagle was drafted in 1899 by the Washington Senators and traded one year later to the Philadelphia Phillies. He played in 1900 with the Phillies but was released in the middle of the 1901 season and picked up by the Boston Braves where he finished off the year. He then joined the Cubs to stay at the beginning of the 1902 season. His first year on the Cubs was also his best year, batting .315 and stealing forty bases. He began 1908 as their starting center fielder before giving way to Hofman later in the year.

He left baseball for good after 1908, living a long life of 83 years and passing away on May 10 of 1956 while living in Chicago.

FACT

His birth name was James Franklin Slagle but was nicknamed 'Rabbit' because of his quickness and ability to steal bases.

STATISTICS

OFFENSE

Career

Games	1,298
Batting Avg	.268
Hits	1,340
Home Runs	2
RBI	344

1908

Games	104
Batting Avg	.222
Hits	78
Home Runs	0
RBI	26

DEFENSE

Career

Games	1,292
Fielding %	.950
Errors	150

1908

Games	101
Fielding %	.976
Errors	5

Frank 'Wildfire' Schulte
Right Field
Born: September 18, 1882
Died: October 2, 1949

Frank Schulte began his major league career as a Cub. His contract with Syracuse of the New York State League was purchased by them late in 1904. He stayed with the Cubs for twelve years, being traded to the Pirates  in the middle of the 1916 season. He finished out that year with the Pirates, moving to the Phillies in mid-1917 and played his last year in the major leagues with the Washington Senators.

He very successfully patrolled right field for the Cubs through all their championship seasons. He was also their cleanup hitter throughout his Cub career, hitting a total of ninety two home runs during his career, a high total during the dead ball era.

Wildfire won the first-ever Most Valuable Player award in 1911. His twenty one home runs that year were the most in the major league in the 1900's thus far.

Ever hear of the 30 30 club, hitting 30 home runs and stealing 30 bases in the same season? He was the founder of that club. Initially he founded the 20 20 20 club, standing for 20 home runs, 20 stolen bases and 20 doubles in the same season. In fact, he also founded the 20 20 20 20 club, adding triples to the mix. Only four players in history have that on their list of accomplishments.

As his skills eroded he finished his last year of major league baseball with the Phillies, Pirates and Senators. He kept playing after that but in the minor leagues, finishing his pro career after the 1923 minor league season.

He had a modestly successful season in 1908, batting .236 with one home run and fifteen stolen bases.

FACT

In addition to being nicknamed 'Rabbit' he was also called 'Shorty' and 'The Human Mosquito' because of his size. He was 5'7" tall.

He stole six bases in the 1907 World Series against the Giants. Setting a record that lasted sixty years. Lou Brock of the St. Louis Cardinals broke the record with seven stolen bases in the 1967 Series against the Red Sox.

STATISTICS

OFFENSE

Career

Games	1,806
Batting Avg	.270
Hits	1,766
Home Runs	92
RBI	792

1908

Games	102
Batting Avg	.236
Hits	91
Home Runs	1
RBI	43

DEFENSE

Career

Games	1,737
Fielding %	.966
Errors	103

1908

Games	102
Fielding %	.994
Errors	1

Solly Hofman
Utility
Born: October 29, 1882
Died: March 10, 1956

Solly Hofman was one of the finest utility players in baseball in the early days. One of his strengths was that he was so versatile. In his career he played first base, second base, third base, shortstop and all three outfield positions. He logged most of his games playing the outfield. He played more games in the outfield than all of the other positions combined.

He made his major league debut with the Pittsburgh Pirates in 1903, playing in just three games with 2 at bats before returning to the minors for 1904. In August of 1904 the Cubs purchased him from Des Moines of the Western League, playing in just seven games through the end of the year. He played a little more the next two years in a utility role before playing in a more major role from 1907 – 1911. It was while with the Cubs until the end of the 1911 season that he played those many positions. It was late in the 1908 season that he began playing mostly outfield. He played center field for Jimmy Slagle beginning in the second half of the season and was a starter in the World Series that year.

He was traded by the Cubs to the Pirates early in the 1912 season and played for them through 1913, going to the minor leagues for the next two years before making a final jump in 1916 first to the Yankees then back to the Cubs to finish out his career. He appeared in just eleven games that year before retiring.

He was generally known as being an excellent fielding outfielder, earning the nickname 'Circus Solly' because of the frequent circus catches he made. 1910 was his best season offensively. He batted .325 and had 86 RBI in 136 games that year.

He never managed and did not make the Hall Of Fame, passing away in St. Louis on March 10, 1956 at the age of 74.

FACTS

He was born Arthur Frederick Hofman.

He was the uncle of Bobby Hofman, a part time player on the New York Giants from 1949-1957.

STATISTICS

OFFENSE

Career

Games	1,194
Batting Avg	.269
Hits	1,095
Home Runs	19
RBI	495

1908

Games	120
Batting Avg	.243
Hits	100
Home Runs	2
RBI	42

DEFENSE

Career

Games	1,175
Fielding %	.966
Errors	169

1908

Games   118

Fielding % By Position:

.955 OF   .972 1B   .941 2B   1.000 3B

Errors   23

Mordecai 'Three Fingers' Brown
Pitcher
Born: October 19, 1876
Died: February 14, 1948

Mordecai Brown was a huge asset for the Cubs, particularly during their championship seasons from 1906 through 1910. He won 29 games in 1908. The last game of the season against the New York Giants was the biggest.

He began his career in 1903 with the St. Louis Cardinals and after one year was traded to the Cubs, playing there from 1904 through the 1912 season. He not only played during their championship seasons but was their best pitcher throughout. His statistically worst season during those years was 1907 when he was 20 – 6 . He went 29 – 9 in 1908 with a 2.35 ERA.

In the last regular season game in 1908 against the Giants he came in with two outs in the 1st inning and two runs scored by the Giants. He shut them down for the rest of the game with the Cubs scoring four runs along the way to earn the victory and the championship. Jack Pfeister started the game but was unable to finish one inning. He finished the year winning two of their four games in the World Series .

He would pitch four more years for the Cubs, finishing 5 – 6 in limited duty in 1912, his last year as a Cub. He did win one more World Series game in 1910 however he lost two.

During his ten years with the Cubs his record was 188 – 86. His total professional record, including two years in the minor leagues in 1914 and 1915, was 239 – 130 with a career ERA of 2.06.

As ace of the Cubs staff he did more than just start games. He was an ace reliever too, as evidenced by the aforementioned game against the Giants when he entered the game with two outs in the first inning. He pitched in relief a total of 130 times throughout his career.

His biggest pitching rival was Christy Mathewson of the Giants. They were matched up against each other in each series the two teams played. Brown won those games more often than he lost with a record of 13 – 12 against Mathewson. He did make a brief appearance with the Cubs in 1916, playing his final game against Mathewson before retiring.

After his retirement from baseball he moved to Terre Haute, Indiana and bought a gas station which he would run for the rest of his life. He passed away in 1948 at 71 years of age, never seeing his election to the Hall Of Fame.

He earned his nickname and style of pitching at age seven when he caught his hand in a corn shredder. Most of his index finger was severed and had to be amputated completely. Later that year be fell and broke his remaining fingers and the middle finger never healed properly. The way he had to grip the ball when pitching, with it resting on his stub and his damaged middle finger gripping it, allowed him to put a tremendous amount of spin on it, resulting in an extraordinary curveball.

FACT

He was angry when he wasn't named starting pitcher in the final game against the Giants in 1908. Jack Pfeister started it because he dominated them that year, earning the nickname 'Jack the Giant Killer'.

STATISTICS

Career

Games	481
Won	239
Lost	130
Innings	3,172.3
ERA	2.06
Strikeouts	1,375

1908

Games	44
Won	29
Lost	9
Innings	312.3
ERA	1.47
Strikeouts	123

Orval 'Orvie' Overall
Pitcher
Born: February 2, 1881
Died: July 14, 1947

Orval Overall played for two teams in his relatively short major league career. He was drafted by the Cincinnati Reds in 1905 and played for them until mid-1906 when he was traded to the Cubs. He remained with  them until he retired in 1910 after a seven year career.

His dominant years came during the championship run. He won twelve games in his first half season for them in 1906, 23 in 1907, 15 in 1908 and 12 in 1910. In 1910, the year they won 104 games but still finished in second place, 6.5 games behind the Pirates, he won 20 games.

In 1908 he started 27 games and pitched in ten more in relief appearances, pitching 225 innings. He ended the season with a ridiculously low 1.92 ERA, which actually was higher than his previous two seasons. He won two games in the Series that year in three appearances. His win in the first game of the series was in relief.

The number of innings he pitched began taking a toll on his arm and he was forced to retire after the 1910 season, pitching with a sore arm throughout the year. He attempted a comeback in 1913 but he was not the pitcher he once was and his comeback was short-lived.

He lived out the rest of his life in California and passed away after a heart attack on July 14, 1947 in Fresno. He was sixty six years old.

STATISTICS

Career

Games	218
Won	108
Lost	71
Innings	1,535.3
ERA	2.23
Strikeouts	935

1908

Games	37
Won	15
Lost	11
Innings	225
ERA	1.92
Strikeouts	167

Ed Reulbach
Pitcher
Born: December 1, 1882
Died: July 17, 1961

Ed Reulbach was a Cub for 8.5 seasons before moving on to Brooklyn, finishing with the Boston Braves. He started with the Cubs in 1905, with his most productive years being from 1905 – 1909. He was very effective for a few years after that however.  He was primarily a starter, pitching very few times in relief in his career. In 1908 he started 35 games and had a 24 – 7 record and a 2.03 ERA. It was his best year. He wasn't his usual productive self in the series that year, not winning a game and giving up 4 runs in 7.2 innings. His career record was 182 – 106 with a very respectable 2.28 ERA.

Ed Reulbach and Mordecai Brown led the way for the Cubs that year, winning 24 and 29 games respectively. Add to that their other starters – Orvie Overall in particular – and you have a dominant pitching staff. Their pitching was their biggest strength during the championship years.

After a poor start in 1913 the Cubs traded him to Brooklyn, where he finished the year with an 8 – 9 record. He stayed with them until 1917, in which he appeared in just five games before retiring.

While he had a successful post-baseball career during which he became a successful lawyer he had a chronically sick son who needed constant care. His son was ill for most of his years before passing away in 1931 at just 21 years old. Reulbach lived for thirty years after that, passing away at 78, but his years after baseball were not very happy because of his unfortunate family situation.

FACTS

On September 26, 1908, Ed Reulbach pitched both games of a double header against Brooklyn. He won both games with complete game shutouts. This during the stretch run for the pennant.

He had a streak of 44 consecutive scoreless innings in late 1908, a record at the time. The current record holder is Orel Hershiser, who threw 59 consecutive scoreless innings with the Dodgers in 1988.

After three good World Series performances in 1906, 1907 and 1908 his performance suffered in 1910, going winless with a 13.05 ERA, giving up three runs in a total of just 2 innings pitched.

He never got elected to the Hall Of Fame, even with career statistics rivaling and even bettering many who are in the Hall now.

STATISTICS

Career

Games	399
Won	182
Lost	106
Innings	2,632.3
ERA	2.28
Strikeouts	1,137

1908

Games	46
Won	24
Lost	7
Innings	297.7
ERA	2.03
Strikeouts	133

Jack Pfeister
Pitcher
Born: May 24, 1878
Died: October 3, 1953

Though technically Jack Pfeister pitched seven full seasons in the major leagues, he only had five years with double digit appearances. His best were 1906 through 1909. Not coincidentally three of those four years the Cubs  made it to the World Series. Evidence of a strong starting staff. His post-season performances weren't the best however, with a career post-season record of 1 – 3 with a 3.97 ERA.

In his four full productive seasons he had a record of 63 wins and 33 losses. He pitched entirely for the Cubs except for a total of six appearances with the Pirates in 1903 and 1904.

Jack Pfeister was a left-handed side-arm pitcher with his most effective pitch being a slow curve. The most important start in his career was against the Giants in the 1908 playoff game but it was not a good one as he only pitched two thirds on an inning and gave up two runs before being relieved by Mordecai Brown. The Giants ended up losing the game 4 – 2 and the Cubs won the N.L. championship.

Jack Pfeister was the pitcher in the game against the Giants known as the Merkle Boner game. This was the game where Fred Merkle was forced out at second when he never touched the base as he thought the game was over. He saw what would have been the game-winning run score on an Al Bridwell single. The game was declared a tie and it enabled the Cubs to go on to the World Series that year. Remarkably, he threw a complete nine inning game with a dislocated tendon in his pitching arm. It hurt so bad he was only able to throw a couple of his sweeping curves, and when he did he had to be helped off the field. He went to the hospital immediately after the game and had the tendon snapped back into place so he could pitch again soon. That helps explain the fact that he only appeared in one game in the World Series and got the team's only loss, giving up seven runs in eight innings.

He pitched only one more complete season, in 1909. He went 17 – 6 but arm troubles forced him to retire after that year. He was thirty three when he retired.

He fell ill with a blood disease in 1953 and had to have his left leg amputated. He died later that year.

FACTS

Jack Pfeister pitched a complete game allowing just five hits on August 30, 1908 against the Giants, winning 2 – 1.

Jack's real name wasn't Pfeister. It was Hagenbush. He remained know as Pfeister and didn't legally change his name until 1950.

The doctor who repaired his tendon in 1908 was named Bonesetter.

Because of how he dominated the Giants during his career he became known as Jack the Giant Killer.

STATISTICS

Career

Games	149
Won	71
Lost	44
Innings	1,067.3
ERA	2.02
Strikeouts	503

1908

Games	33
Won	12
Lost	10
Innings	252
ERA	2.00
Strikeouts	117

Chick Fraser
Pitcher
Born: August 26, 1873
Died: May 8, 1940

Although Chick Fraser had respectable years in 1899, 1900 and 1901 he was for the most part a journeyman pitcher who played for twelve years in the major leagues. Two of those years were partial seasons. He spent his last three uneventful  years on the Cubs, one of them his last year in baseball – 1909. He appeared in just one game that year, on May third, pitching three innings. He gave up one unearned run in that game, calling it quits shortly afterwards. His career record was 175 – 212.

His first year in the major leagues was 1898. He was picked up by the soon to be defunct Cleveland Spiders in the middle of the season. He won twenty games twice in his career, in 1899 and 1901. 1900 was his only other winning season.

He played for seven teams in twelve years, playing for the Phillies twice so technically he played for six teams. Those teams were the Cleveland Spiders, Philadelphia Phillies, Philadelphia Athletics, the Phillies again, the Boston Beaneaters (Red Sox), Cincinnati Reds and Chicago Cubs.

He was not one of the stars on the 1908 Cubs but was a serviceable pitcher, appearing in twenty six games. In seventeen of those games he was a starter, compiling an 11 – 9 record. He did not make an appearance in the World Series.

He passed away at 66 on May 8, 1940 in Wendell, Ohio.

FACTS

Fraser led the league in hit batters twice, 1898 and 1899. He hit 29 in 1898 and 22 in 1899.

In 1901 and 1905 he was among the league leaders in complete games pitched with thirty five each year.

On June 16, 1903 with the Phillies he hit a game winning home run against the Giants.

STATISTICS

Career

Games	433
Won	175
Lost	212
Innings	3,356
ERA	3.68
Strikeouts	1089

1908

Games	26
Won	11
Lost	9
Innings	162.7
ERA	2.27
Strikeouts	66

Carl Lundgren
Pitcher
Born: February 16, 1880
Died: August 21, 1934

Carl Lundgren played his entire career on the Cubs, joining them in June 1902 and playing until the beginning of 1909. He spent his career as a starting pitcher. Like Chick Fraser he was not a star on the 1908 team but a serviceable  addition to a very good staff. The Cubs were his hometown team. He lived his entire life nearby with his hometown being Marengo, Illinois. He lived there until his death in 1934.

He finished with a winning record in the major leagues at 91 – 55 and an ERA of 2.42. Although he spent his time with a very successful team his low ERA shows that he was a good pitcher on that team.

In 1908 his career took a downturn. He posted his only full season losing record at 6 – 9 with an ERA of 4.22, pitching in just 23 games. He was a part-time starter that year.

Upon his retirement after the 1909 season he did not move on to the minor leagues to continue playing as was common at the time. He became a college basketball coach at the University of Michigan, passing away at 54 years old.

FACTS

He never had a twenty win season, although in 1904, 1906 and 1907 he posted 17, 17 and 18 win seasons respectively. His lowest ERA was in the 1907 season – 1.17. That was the year of his highest win total of 18.

STATISTICS

Career

Games	179
Won	91
Lost	55
Innings	1,322
ERA	2.42
Strikeouts	535

1908

Games	23
Won	6
Lost	9
Innings	138.2
ERA	4.22
Strikeouts	38

THE REST OF THE ROSTER

Pat Moran
Catcher
Born: February 7, 1876
Died: March 7, 1924

Pat Moran was backup catcher to Johnny Kling in 1908. He began his career in 1901 with the Boston Beaneaters (Braves). His two biggest years were 1903 and 1904, the only two years with more than one hundred games played. He was  traded to the Cubs after the 1905 season, playing for them through 1909. He finished his career in mid 1914 with the Philadelphia Phillies. He had very limited playing time his last three years, playing a total of fifteen games those years. Other than 1903 and 1904 he was strictly a backup.

After his playing career he became a manager. First he was manager of the Phillies from 1915 – 1918, then manager of the Reds from 1919 – 1923.

He appeared in two World Series as a manager, once with the Phillies in 1915 and then with the Reds in 1919, the year of the Black Sox scandal.

The 1919 World Series was one of the most memorable of all time, but not because of Moran's team's victory. Most people would be hard-pressed to name the team the White Sox faced in the year of the gambling scandal but the Series will always be remembered.

1923 was his last season as a manager. The Reds finished second that year. He passed away in March of 1924, falling victim to Bright's Disease, a kidney sickness. He was succeeded by Jack Hendricks as manager of the Reds.

STATISTICS

OFFENSE

Career

Games	818
Batting Avg	.235
Hits	618
Home Runs	18
RBI	262

1908

Games	50
Batting Avg	.260
Hits	39
Home Runs	0
RBI	12

DEFENSE

Career

Games	767
Fielding %	.972
Errors	135

1908

Games	45
Fielding %	.968
Errors	10

Doc Marshall
Catcher
Born: September 22, 1875
Died: December 11, 1959

Doc Marshall was the Cub's third string catcher in 1908. They acquired him from the Cardinals in May and he played in twelve games that year.

His career began in 1904 with the Phillies. He played with six teams, retiring after the 1909 season. The most games he appeared in in one season was eighty four, in 1907 with the Cardinals.

He was a well-traveled player, playing with the Phillies, Giants, Braves, Cardinals, Cubs and Superbas (Dodgers). He had just twenty at bats for the Cubs in 1908 and didn't make an appearance in the World Series..

He passed away in 1959 in Clinton, Illinois at the age of 84.

STATISTICS

OFFENSE

Career

Games	261
Batting Avg	.210
Hits	159
Home Runs	2
RBI	54

1908 (Cubs)

Games	12
Batting Avg	.300
Hits	1
Home Runs	0
RBI	1

DEFENSE

Career

Games	213
Fielding %	.961
Errors	51

1908 (Cubs)

Games	7
Fielding %	.969
Errors	1

Del Howard
1B/OF
Born: December 24, 1877
Died: December 24, 1956

Del Howard played for five years for the Pirates, Braves and Cubs. He played both first base and all three outfield positions. Howard played in over one hundred games his first three years, ending with sixty nine games in 1909, his final year. He also pitched in a game in 1905 with the Pirates, not getting a decision after six innings pitched.

He passed away on his birthday in 1956 at 79 years of age.

STATISTICS

<u>OFFENSE</u>

<u>Career</u>

Games	536
Batting Avg	.263
Hits	482
Home Runs	6
RBI	193

<u>1908</u>

Games	96
Batting Avg	.279
Hits	88
Home Runs	1
RBI	26

<u>DEFENSE</u>

<u>Career</u>

Games	499
Fielding %	.965
Errors	96

<u>1908</u>

Games	86
Fielding %	. 965
Errors	6

Pitching

Games	1
Won	0
Lost	0
Innings	6
ERA	0.00
Strikeouts	0

Heinie Zimmerman
2B, 3B, SS, OF
Born: February 9, 1887
Died: March 11, 1969

Heinie Zimmerman played for thirteen years, starting with the Cubs in 1907 and finishing with the Giants. He played for the Cubs for nine years, being traded to the Giants in the middle of 1916.

His best year was 1912 when he led the National League in batting average and home runs, narrowly missing winning the Triple Crown. Honus Wagner led the league in RBIs. With the Cubs in 1908 he played second, third, shortstop and all three outfield positions, appearing in thirty games. His final year – 1919 – he got suspended under suspicion of trying to convince people to fix games. This was unrelated to the Black Sox controversy of that year.

He spent his retired years in New York, passing away there in 1969 at age eighty two.

STATISTICS

OFFENSE

Career

Games	1,456
Batting Avg	.295
Hits	1,566
Home Runs	58
RBI	796
Stolen Bases	175

1908

Games	46
Batting Avg	.292
Hits	33
Home Runs	0
RBI	9

DEFENSE

Career

Games	1,401
Fielding %	.933
Errors	381

1908

Games	30
Fielding %	.923
Errors	9

Kid Durbin
Outfield
Born: September 10, 1886
Died: September 11, 1943

Kid Durbin played for three years in the majors, starting with the Cubs in 1907. After playing for the Cubs for two years he played for the Reds and Pirates in 1909 before retiring from baseball.

In 1908 he appeared in fourteen games, playing eleven of them in center field. He pinch hit in the other three games. In his career he had fifty one at-bats.

He passed away in 1943 at 57 years of age.

STATISTICS

OFFENSE

Career

Games	32
Batting Avg	.275
Hits	14
Home Runs	0
RBI	0
Stolen Bases	0

1908

Games	14
Batting Avg	.250
Hits	7
Home Runs	0
RBI	0

DEFENSE

Career

Games	19
Fielding %	1.000
Errors	0

1908

Games	14
Fielding %	1.000
Errors	0

Jack Hayden
Outfield
Born: October 21, 1880
Died: August 3, 1942

No Picture Available

Jack Hayden played major league baseball for three years, beginning in 1901 and finishing in 1908. 1901, 1906 and 1908 were the three years he played. In 1908, he played in right field in parts of 11 games. He lived 62 years, passing away in August 1942.

STATISTICS

OFFENSE

Career

Games	147
Batting Avg	.251
Hits	145
Home Runs	1
RBI	33

1908

Games	11
Batting Avg	.200
Hits	9
Home Runs	0
RBI	2

DEFENSE

Career

Games	146
Fielding %	.929
Errors	18

1908

Games	11
Fielding %	1.000
Errors	0

Vin Campbell
Outfield
Born: January 30, 1888
Died: November 16, 1969

Vin Campbell played for six years, taking 1909 and 1913 off. He played in one game in 1908 for the Cubs, pinch hitting but not playing in the field. He had one at-bat. His final two years, 1914 and 1915, were spent in the minor leagues.

He died in Maryland in 1969 at eighty one.

STATISTICS

<u>OFFENSE</u>

<u>Career</u>

Games	546
Batting Avg	.310
Hits	642
Home Runs	15
RBI	167

<u>1908</u>

Games	1
Batting Avg	0
Hits	0
Home Runs	0
RBI	0

<u>DEFENSE</u>

<u>Career</u>

Games	497
Fielding %	.929
Errors	76

<u>1908</u>

Games	1
Fielding %	0
Errors	0

Andy Coakley
Pitcher
Born: November 20, 1882
Died: September 27, 1963

Andy Coakley played for four teams in eight years. He began with the Philadelphia Athletics, playing for them for five years before spending a year each on the Reds, Cubs and Highlanders (Yankees), retiring after the 1911 season.

He played in four games for the Cubs in 1908 and one in 1909. He was 2 – 0 in 1908 with a 0.89 ERA.

He passed away in 1963 at eighty.

STATISTICS

Career

Games	150
Won	58
Lost	59
Innings	1,072.3
ERA	2.35
Strikeouts	428

1908

Games	4
Won	2
Lost	0
Innings	20.3
ERA	0.89
Strikeouts	7

Floyd 'Rube' Kroh
Pitcher
Born: August 25, 1886
Died: March 17, 1944

Rube Kroh played for three teams in six years. In 1908 with the Cubs he pitched in two games, going 0 – 0. He began with the Red Sox in 1906, went to the Cubs in 1908 and finished with the Braves in 1912. He did not play in 1911.

He passed away in 1944 at fifty seven.

FACT

On September 21, 1908, Floyd Kroh pitched eight innings against the Phillies, giving up just one run. The Cubs won in ten innings 2 – 1 on a sacrifice fly by Orvie Overall.

STATISTICS

Career

Games	36
Won	14
Lost	9
Innings	216.3
ERA	2.20
Strikeouts	92

1908

Games	2
Won	0
Lost	0
Innings	12.0
ERA	1.50
Strikeouts	11

Carl Spongberg
Pitcher
Born: May 21, 1884
Died: July 21, 1938

No Picture Available

Carl Spongberg played baseball for one year – 1908 - with the Cubs.   He played in one game, pitching seven innings. He passed away in 1938 at 54.

STATISTICS

Career

Games	1
Won	0
Lost	0
Innings	7.0
ERA	9.00
Strikeouts	4

1908

Games	1
Won	0
Lost	0
Innings	7.0
ERA	9.00
Strikeouts	4

Bill Mack
Pitcher
Born: February 12, 1885
Died: September 30, 1971

No Picture Available

Bill Mack played one year – 1908. He appeared in two games for the Cubs and that comprised his entire career. He pitched six innings in two games with no record.

He lived to be 86, passing away in 1971.

STATISTICS

Career

Games	2
Won	0
Lost	0
Innings	6.0
ERA	3.00
Strikeouts	2

1908

Games	2
Won	0
Lost	0
Innings	6.0
ERA	3.00
Strikeouts	2

CUBS START RACE WITH VICTORY, 6-5.

New Reds Gain Big Early Lead, but Champs Chop It Down and Win.

CROWD OF 19,000 AT GAME.

"Heinie" Zimmerman Busts Tie with Hit in Ninth; Greatest Opener Yet in "Cincy."

THE OPENING DAY GAME

The Cubs opened 1908 with a 6 – 5 win over the Cincinnati Reds on a rainy day on April 14th. Orvie Overall got the win with Mordecai 'Three Fingers' Brown putting the Reds down in the ninth.

Going into the top of the ninth the game was tied at 5 – 5. Being the visiting team the Cubs batted first. With two outs and Johnny Evers on second pinch hitter Heinie Zimmerman drove Evers in with a single over second base. He was thrown out at second trying to stretch it into a double but the damage was done. The Cubs led 6 – 5 with Three Fingers set to pitch the bottom half of the inning. He shut them down and the Cubs had their first win.

The Reds did manage a hit off Brown though. Larry McLean led off with a single while pinch hitting for pitcher Billy Campbell. He was thrown out trying to stretch it into a double much as Zimmerman was in the top of the inning. Brown cruised the rest of the way.

The opening day lineup for the Cubs:

Jimmy Slagle	CF
Jimmy Sheckard	LF
Wildfire Schulte	RF
Frank Chance	1B
Harry Steinfeldt	3B
Johnny Evers	2B
Joe Tinker	SS
Johnny Kling	C
Orvie Overall	P

CHICAGO.

	AB	R	BH	TB	BB	SH	SB	PO	A	E
Slagle, cf.....	3	1	0	0	1	0	0	1	0	1
Sheckard, lf..	4	0	0	0	0	0	0	0	0	0
Schulte, rf....	4	0	1	1	0	0	1	2	0	0
Chance, 1b.....	3	0	1	1	1	0	0	9	0	0
Steinfeldt, 3b.	4	1	1	3	0	0	0	3	3	0
Evers, 2b.....	3	3	3	4	1	0	0	6	4	0
Tinker, ss.....	2	1	1	1	0	2	0	2	3	0
Kling, c.......	4	0	2	2	0	0	0	4	2	1
Overall, p....	3	0	1	1	0	0	0	0	1	1
Brown, p.....	0	0	0	0	0	0	0	0	0	0
*Zimmerman.	1	0	1	1	0	0	0	0	0	0
Totals....31		6	11	14	3	2	1	27	13	3

*Batted for Overall in ninth.

CINCINNATI.

	AB	R	BH	TB	BB	SH	SB	PO	A	E
Huggins, 2b..	4	1	1	1	1	0	1	4	3	0
Lobert, lf.....	4	1	1	1	0	1	1	6	0	0
Mitchell, rf...	3	1	0	0	0	1	0	0	0	0
Ganzel, 1b....	4	1	1	1	0	0	0	9	0	0
Schlei, c......	3	1	2	2	1	0	0	7	2	0
Mowrey, 3b..	4	0	2	2	0	0	1	0	1	0
Paskert, cf...	3	0	0	0	1	0	0	1	2	0
Hulswitt, ss..	3	0	0	0	1	0	0	0	0	0
Ewing, p.....	0	0	0	0	1	0	0	0	4	0
Campbell, p..	1	0	0	0	0	0	0	0	4	0
†McLean.....	1	0	1	1	0	0	0	0	0	0
‡Kane.......	0	0	0	0	0	0	1	0	0	0
Totals....31		5	8	8	5	2	4	27	12	0

†Ran for Ewing in fourth. ‡Batted for Campbell in ninth.

Chicago ....0 2 0 1 1 1 0 0 1—6
Cincinnati ....5 0 0 0 0 0 0 0 0—5

Two base hit—Evers. Three base hit—Steinfeldt. Struck out—By Ewing, 2; by Campbell, 8; by Overall, 4. Bases on balls—Off Ewing, 1; off Campbell, 2; off Overall, 5. Double plays—Hulswitt-Huggins-Ganzel; Huggins-Ganzel. Left on bases—Chicago, 8; Cincinnati, 6. Wild pitch—Ewing. Time 1:55. Umpire—O'Day. Attendance, 19,257.

THE MERKLE BONER GAME

CHICAGO CUBS VS NEW YORK GIANTS

WEDNESDAY SEPTEMBER 23, 1908

BLUNDER COSTS GIANTS VICTORY

Merkle Rushes Off Base Line Before Winning Run Is Scored, and Is Declared Out.

CONFUSION ON BALL FIELD

Chance Asserts That McCormick's Run Does Not Count— Crowd Breaks Up Game.

UMPIRE DECLARES IT A TIE

Wednesday September 23, 1908 is the day that effectively decided the championship of the National League. The game that day between the Cubs and Giants was declared a tie causing the two teams to be tied for first at the end of the regular season. The makeup of this game decided the championship.

The game on the 23rd is often referred to as the 'Merkle Boner' game due to Fred Merkle's baserunning gaffe that caused the game to be declared a 1 -1 tie.

Until the controversial play at the end the game had been a tight pitcher's duel. Jack Pfeister pitched a nine inning five hitter and the Giant's Christy Mathewson a seven hitter. Nine of the twenty seven outs recorded by Mathewson were by strikeout.

The game was scoreless until the fifth inning when the Cubs scored their lone run. With one out Joe Tinker drove the ball to right-center for a double. When attempting to field the ball, however, Giant right fielder Mike Donlin accidently kicked it for a two base error allowing Tinker to score. Rather than being considered a home run by Tinker it was scored as a double and two-base error by Donlin.

The score was Cubs 1 Giants 0 after five innings.

The Giants scored a run of their own in the sixth. Buck Herzog led off the Giants sixth with a ground ball to Harry Steinfeldt at third. Steinfeldt threw the ball over first baseman Frank Chance's head, allowing Herzog to advance to second.

Giants catcher Roger Bresnahan followed with a sacrifice bunt to move Herzog to third and Mike Donlin redeemed himself for his fielding error in the previous inning by lining a single over second base to center scoring Herzog.

The score was now Cubs 1 Giants 1 after six innings.

The game was scoreless from then on until the bottom of the ninth. With the score still tied at one with one out in the inning Giant third baseman Art Devlin singled to center. Moose McCormick grounded to Johnny Evers who forced Donlin at second. Two outs. Fred Merkle at bat. Merkle singled and McCormick advanced to third. Al Bridwell was next at bat and he singled to center to score McCormick with the winning run. The fans stormed the field in celebration but in the excitement Fred Merkle never bothered to advance all the way to second, instead turning to run to the Giant clubhouse thinking the game had ended.

Johnny Evers saw this and called for the ball to be thrown to second to force Merkle, which would end the game before the run officially scored. Frank Chance ran to cover second but before the throw could reach him the ball was intercepted by Giant pitcher Joe McGinnity, who threw it into the crowd in celebration before Chance could complete the force.

Being the Cub manager, Chance appealed to umpire Frank O'Day for an immediate ruling. After a short period of time O'Day ruled Merkle out at second with the run not counting. When the crowd, who had been mobbing the field in celebration, got wind of this the police had to be brought in to keep them under control and protect O'Day. The fans could not be calmed so the game could not continue and was declared a tie.

Chicago filed a protest the next day claiming the Giants should forfeit the game for not showing up the next day to play as they wanted them to. The Giants and New York sportswriters still declared the game a victory for the Giants. League president Harry Pulliam put all questions to rest on October second when he supported his umpire and officially declared the game a tie, leading to the eventual playoff game which the Cubs won.

THE RULE

One run shall be scored every time a base runner, after having legally touched the first three bases, shall legally touch the home base before three men are put out, provided, however, that if he reach home on or during a play in which the third man be forced out or be put out before reaching first base a run shall not count. A force-out can be made only when a base runner legally loses the right to the base he occupies and is thereby obliged to advance as the result of a fair hit ball not caught on the fly.

THE BOX SCORE

CHICAGO.	AB	R	H	PO	A		NEW YORK.	AB	R	H	PO	A
Hayden, rf.	4	0	0	1	0		Herzog, 2b.	3	1	1	1	1
Total...	30	1	5*27	15			Bres'h'n, c.	3	0	0	10	0
Schulte, lf.	4	0	0	1	0		Donlin, rf.	4	0	1	2	0
Chance, 1b.	4	0	1	11	1		Seymour, cf.	4	0	1	1	0
St'nf'dt, 3b.	2	0	0	1	0		Devlin, 3b.	4	0	2	0	2
Hofman, cf.	3	0	1	0	0		McC'm'k, lf.	3	0	0	1	0
Tinker, ss.	3	1	1	8	6		Merkle, 1b.	3	0	1	10	1
Kling, c....	3	0	1	0	1		B'dwell, ss.	4	0	1	2	3
Pfeister, p.	3	0	0	1	0		M'th's'n, p.	3	0	0	0	2
Total...	30	1	5	27	13		Total...	31	1	7	27	0

Errors—Steinfeldt, Tinker, (2.)

Chicago ....0 0 0 0 1 0 0 0 0—1
New York ....0 0 0 0 1 0 0 0 0—1

Home run—Tinker. Sacrifice hits—Steinfeldt, Bresnahan. Double plays—Tinker and Chance, (2;) Evers and Chance; Mathewson, Bridwell, and Merkle. Left on bases—New York, 7; Chicago, 3. First base on balls—Off Pfeister, 2. First base on errors—New York, 2. Hit by pitcher—By Pfeister, 1. Struck out—By Pfeister, none; by Mathewson, 9. Time of game—One hour and thirty minutes. Umpires—Messrs. O'Day and Emslie.

8
THE PLAYOFF GAME

On October 8, the Cubs played the Giants on the final day of the season to decide first place in the National League. The headline on the following page says it all, including the fact that a fan was killed beforehand trying to find a suitable place to watch the game from outside the Polo Grounds. The Polo Grounds were sold out and thousands of fans lined the streets looking for any opportunity they could to be able to see what was going on inside. A crowd flocked to the elevated tracks behind the stadium to see and one man fell backward onto the third rail electrocuting himself. His place was immediately replaced by another anxious fan as a good vantage point from which to watch.

The Cubs won the game 4 – 2, scoring all four runs in the fourth inning on RBI's by Johnny Kling, Frank Schulte and two by Frank Chance.

Mordecai Brown got the victory, pitching eight and a third innings of four-hit baseball, giving up just two runs. Jack Pfeister got the final two outs.

THE CUBS WIN
THE PENNANT

Hit Mathewson for Four Runs in Third Inning of Decisive Game and Beat the Giants.

GIANTS SCORE TWO RUNS

"Three-Fingered" Brown, Chicago's Star Twirler, Has Home Team at His Mercy.

40,000 SEE GREAT CONTEST

Probably as Many More Shut Out— Wall Street Left Outside—One Would-Be Spectator Killed by a Fall.

THE BOX SCORE

CHICAGO.	AB	R	H	PO	A	NEW YORK.	AB	R	H	PO	A
Sheck'd, lf.	4	0	0	4	0	Tenney, 1b.	2	1	1	9	0
Evers, 2b.	3	1	1	0	3	Herzog, 2b.	3	0	0	1	2
Schulte, rf.	4	1	1	4	0	Bres'h'n, c.	4	0	1	10	2
Chance, 1b.	4	0	3	13	0	Donlin, rf.	4	0	1	0	0
St'nf'dt, 3b.	4	0	1	0	3	Seym'r, cf.	3	0	0	2	0
Hofm'n, cf.	0	0	0	0	0	Devlin, 3b.	4	1	1	2	0
Howard, cf.	4	0	0	1	0	McC'm'k, lf.	4	0	1	3	1
Tinker, ss.	4	1	1	1	4	B'dwell, ss.	3	0	0	0	1
Kling, c.	3	1	1	4	1	M'th'son, p.	2	0	0	0	3
Pfeister, p.	0	0	0	0	0	*Doyle	1	0	0	0	0
Brown, p.	2	0	0	0	1	Wiltse, p.	0	0	0	0	0
Total...	32	4	8	27	12	Total...	30	2	5	27	9

Error—Tenney.
*Batted for Mathewson in seventh inning.

```
Chicago ...............0  0  4  0  0  0  0  0  0—4
New York .............1  0  0  0  0  0  1  0  0—2
```

Two-base hits—Donlin, Schulte, Chance, Evers. Three-base hit—Tinker. Hits—Off Pfeister, 1 in two-thirds of an inning; off Brown, 4 in eight and one-third innings; off Mathewson, 7 in seven innings; off Wiltse, 1 in two innings. Sacrifice hits—Tenney, Brown. Double plays—Kling and Chance, McCormick and Bresnahan. Left on bases—Chicago, 3; New York, 6. First base on balls—Off Pfeister, 2; off Brown, 1; off Mathewson, 1. First base on error—Chicago. Hit by pitcher—By Pfeister, 1. Struck out—By Mathewson, 7; by Wiltse, 2; by Pfeister, 1; by Brown, 1. Time of game—One hour and forty minutes. Umpires—Messrs. Johnstone and Klem.

107

9
THE SEASON

The Cubs finished the season with a 99-55 record. The New York Giants were one game behind at 98-56 in a tie with the Pittsburgh Pirates. It was the Giants and not the Pirates who nearly won the crown, with the last game of the season being won the Cubs. The last game of the season was the one that had to be played because of the Merkle Boner game that ended in a tie rather than the Giants getting the victory, which they have had if Fred Merkle had touched second base when Al Bridwell hit the potentially game winning single instead of turning to run to the clubhouse. That game was declared a tie afterwards because rioting fans would not get off the field to allow the game to continue. If not for Johnny Ever's quick thinking about forcing Merkle at second the Cubs wouldn't have made it to the World Series.

In 1908, including the World Series, the Cubs played a total of 158 games, hit nineteen home runs, batted .249 and scored a total of 624 runs. They did not lead the league in any of those categories.

Their pitchers wound up with a 2.14 ERA. Again, not first in the league. The winningest pitcher was Mordecai Brown with twenty nine wins to go along with nineteen losses. Together with Ed Reulbach's twenty four wins they accounted for more than half the Cubs ninety nine wins that season. The rest of the pitcher's wins came from Orvie Overall with fifteen, Jack Pfeister with twelve, Chick Fraser with eleven and Carl Lundgren with six. The bullpen had a total of two victories.

Their low point came on August sixteenth when they were in third place, six games behind the leader.

They may not have led the league in any offensive categories but it was enough to win first place and go on to World Series victory

Season attendance was 665,325.

THE STANDINGS

TEAM	W	L	PCT.	GB
Chicago Cubs	99	55	.643	--
New York Giants	98	56	.636	1
Pittsburgh Pirates	98	56	.636	1
Philadelphia Phillies	83	71	.539	16
Cincinnati Reds	73	81	.474	26
Boston Doves	63	91	.409	36
Brooklyn Superbas	53	101	.344	46
St. Louis Cardinals	49	105	.318	50

CUBS AND TIGERS READY FOR BATTLE

First Game of World's Baseball Championship to be Played To-day at Detroit.

The Chicago Cubs defeated the Detroit Tigers four games to one in the 1908 World Series. They won the first two games, lost the third and won games four and five for the championship. The final results:

Game One:
Cubs 10 Tigers 6 WP Mordecai Brown LP Ed Summers

Game Two:
Cubs 6 Tigers 1 WP Orvie Overall LP Bill Donovan

Game Three:
Tigers 8 Cubs 3 WP George Mullin LP Jack Pfeister

Game Four:
Cubs 3 Tigers 0 WP Mordecai Brown LP Ed Summers

Game Five:
Cubs 2 Tigers 0 WP Orvie Overall LP Bill Donovan

Total attendance for the series was 62,232. 29,929 in Detroit and 32,303 in Chicago. Capacity at each park was 8,500 at Bennett Park in Detroit and 16,000 at the West Side Grounds in Chicago. The smallest crowd ever to attend a World Series game was game five in Detroit where just 6,210 attended.

CUBS EARN A VICTORY OVER TIGERS ON A MUDDY FIELD

First Game In World's Series Marred by Rain—Chance Outgenerals Jennings in the Matter of Handling His Pitchers in Cold and Wet Weather.

SCORING RUNDOWN

INNING ONE:
The Cubs were held scoreless in the top of the first but the Tigers came through in their half , scoring one run on a Ty Cobb single.
Tigers 1 Cubs 0

INNING TWO:
No runs scored.

INNING THREE:
The Cubs get on the board with four. Runs driven in by Frank Schulte, Harry Steinfeldt and Joe Tinker with an unearned run scoring on an error by shortstop Germany Schaefer.
Cubs 4 Tigers 1

Innings 4, 5 and 6 were scoreless.

INNING SEVEN:
The Cubs score a run in the top of the seventh on a sacrifice fly by Harry Steinfeldt while the Tigers scored three on RBI's by Boss Schmidt, Red Downs and pitcher Ed Summers. Orvie Overall came on in relief of Ed Reulbach to end the inning.
Cubs 5 Tigers 4

INNING EIGHT:
Mordecai Brown comes on in relief of Overall and allows the Tigers to score two on a single by Claude Rossman, with an error by Johnny Evers allowing the second run to score on that hit.
Tigers 6 Cubs 5

INNING NINE:
The Cubs bust out with five runs. Cub RBI's by Solly Hofman (2), Joe Tinker and Johnny Kling (2).
Cubs 10 Tigers 6

FINAL SCORE

Cubs 10 Tigers 6

THE BOX SCORE

DETROIT.						CHICAGO.					
	A B	R	H	PO	A		A B	R	H	PO	A
M'Int're. lf.	3	1	2	3	0	Sheck'd. lf.	6	1	3	1	1
O'Leary. ss.	4	0	1	1	3	Evers. 2b...	4	1	2	2	2
Crawf'd. cf.	4	1	0	4	0	Schulte. rf.	4	2	2	1	0
Cobb. rf...	4	2	2	0	0	Chance. 1b.	4	2	1	12	0
R'sman. 1b.	4	1	2	12	0	St'nf'dt. 3b.	3	2	2	0	0
Sch'fer. 3b.	3	0	0	1	2	Hofman. cf.	4	1	1	4	1
Schmidt. c.	4	0	0	4	1	Tinker. ss..	5	1	2	0	4
Downs. 2b.	4	1	1	2	4	Kling. c...	3	0	1	7	1
Killian. p..	0	0	0	0	1	R'lbach. p.	4	0	0	0	4
Sum'rs. p...	3	0	1	0	5	Overall. p..	1	0	0	0	0
*Thomas ..	1	0	1	0	0	Brown. p..	0	0	0	0	2
†Jones	1	0	0	0	0						
‡Winter ...	0	0	0	0	0	Total...38	10	14	27	15	

Total...35 6 10 27 16

*Batted for O'Leary in ninth inning.
†Batted for Summers in ninth inning.
‡Ran for Thomas in ninth inning.
Errors—Chance. Steinfeldt, McIntyre, Schaefer, Downs.

Detroit	1	0	0	0	0	0	3	2	0—	6
Chicago	0	0	4	0	0	0	1	0	5—	10

Hits—Off Killian, 5 in two and one-third innings; off Summers, 9 in six and two-third innings; off Reulbach, 8 in six and two-thirds innings; off Overall, 0 in one-third innings; off Brown, 2 in two innings. Two-base hits—Downs, Sheckard, (2.) Sacrifice hits—Cobb, Schaefer, Evers. Schulte. Steinfeldt, Kling, Brown. Stolen bases—McIntyre, Chance, Hofman, Tinker, (3.) First base on balls—Off Killian, 3; off Summers, 1; off Overall, 1; off Brown, 1. Hit by pitcher—By Overall. 1. First base on errors—Detroit, 1; Chicago, 2. Left on bases—Detroit, 7; Chicago, 9. Struck out—By Killian, 1; by Summers, 2; by Reulbach, 5; by Brown, 1. Wild pitch—Brown. Time of game—Two hours and ten minutes. Umpires—Messrs. Sheridan and O'Day. Attendance, 10,812.

114

DONOVAN WEAKENS AND CHICAGO WINS

World's Champions Score Six Runs In Eighth Inning and Take Second Game.

OVERALL IN FINE FORM

Cub Pitcher Holds Detroit Down to Four Hits — Speculators Lose Money—Final Score 6—1.

SCORING RUNDOWN

The game was a pitcher's duel until the top of the eighth when the Cubs registered six runs on six hits, including a two-run homer by Johnny Tinker. The Tigers scored in the ninth giving the Cubs a 6 – 1 victory and 2 – 0 lead in the series.

Neither pitcher allowed a hit in the first half of the game. The Tigers got their first hit in the fifth inning while the Cubs waited until the sixth to record their first on a single by Overall himself. Both pitchers pitched complete games. Overall allowed four hits and Donovan seven.

FINAL SCORE

Cubs 6 Tigers 1

THE BOX SCORE

CHICAGO.	AB	R	H	PO	A	DETROIT.	AB	R	H	PO	A
Sh'kard, lf.	4	1	1	3	0	M'Int're, lf.	4	0	0	3	0
Evers, 2b..	4	1	1	0	6	O'Leary, ss.	3	0	0	1	1
Schulte, .rf.	4	1	1	1	0	Crawf'd, cf.	4	0	0	4	0
Chance, 1b.	3	0	0	12	1	Cobb, rf....	4	0	1	1	0
St'nf'dt, 3b.	4	0	0	1	1	R'ssm'n,1b.	4	0	0	8	1
Hofman, cf.	3	1	1	0	0	Sch'fer, 3b.	3	0	2	0	1
Tinker, ss..	3	1	1	2	3	Schmidt, c.	3	0	1	7	0
Kling, c...	3	1	1	8	0	Downs, 2b..	2	0	0	0	4
Overall, p..	3	0	1	0	3	Don'van, p.	2	0	0	0	1
						*Jones	0	1	0	0	0
Total...	31	6	7	27	14	Total...	29	1	4	24	8

*Batted for O'Leary in ninth inning.
Errors—Tinker, Donovan.
Chicago ....0 0 0 0 0 0 0 6 ..—6
Detroit ....0 0 0 0 0 0 0 0 1—1
Two-base hit—Kling. Three-base hit—Schulte.
Home run—Tinker. Sacrifice hit—Donovan.
Stolen bases—Sheckard, Evers, Chance. Double
plays—Tinker and Chance; Downs, O'Leary, and
Rossman. Left on bases—Chicago, 2; Detroit,
4. First base on balls—Off Overall, 2; off
Donovan, 1. First base on errors—Chicago, 1.
Struck out—By Overall, 5; by Donovan, 7. Wild
pitch—Donovan. Time of game—One hour and
twenty-four minutes. Umpires—Messrs. Klem
and Connolly. Attendance, (official)—17,760.

TIGERS PULL CUBS DOWN TO DEFEAT

Heavy Batting in Sixth Inning Turns Tide for Detroit in World's Series.

MULLIN PUZZLES CHICAGO

World's Champions Rudely Shaken Up by Terrific Cannonading of American League Batsmen.

SCORING RUNDOWN

INNING ONE:
The game started out quickly with the Tigers scoring a run in the top of the first on a single by Ty Cobb.
Tigers 1 Cubs 0

Innings two and three were scoreless.

INNING FOUR:
The Cubs came up with three unearned runs. Johnny Evers walked and advanced to second on an error by Claude Rossman then scored on a single by Frank Chance. Chance then stole second and scored when Bill Coughlin errored on a Harry Steinfeldt hit. Solly Hofman tripled, driving in Steinfeldt for another unearned run.
Cubs 3 Tigers 1

INNING SIX:
After a quiet fifth inning the Tigers brought home five in the top of the sixth. With two men on George Mullin scored on a Sam Crawford single. Ty Cobb drove in Matty McIntyre followed by a Claude Rossman single driving in Charley O'Leary and Crawford. Lastly, Ira Thomas doubled in Rossman for their fifth run of the inning.
Tigers 6 Cubs 3

INNING EIGHT:

The Tigers scored two more on a Coughlin sacrifice fly and a Mullin single for the final two runs of the game.

Tigers 8 Cubs 3

FINAL SCORE

Tigers 8 Cubs 3

THE BOX SCORE

DETROIT.	AB	R	H	PO	A	CHICAGO.	AB	R	H	PO	A
McIntyre, lf.	4	1	1	1	0	Sheck'd, lf.	4	0	0	1	0
O'Leary, ss.	5	2	2	1	3	Evers, 2b.	3	1	0	1	6
Crawf,d, cf.	5	1	2	3	0	Schulte, rf.	4	0	1	1	0
Cobb, rf.	5	1	4	0	0	Chance, 1b.	4	1	2	14	0
Rossm'n,1b.	4	2	2	8	0	Steinf't, 3b.	4	1	1	1	4
Sch'f'r, 2b.	4	0	0	4	4	Hofman, cf.	4	0	2	3	1
Thomas, c.	3	0	1	10	2	Tinker, ss.	3	0	1	3	1
C'ghlin, 3b.	4	0	0	0	1	Kling, c.	3	0	0	3	2
Mullin, p.	3	1	1	0	2	Pfeister, p.	2	0	0	0	0
						Reulbach, p.	0	0	0	0	1
Total	37	8	13	27	12	*Howard	1	0	0	0	0
						Total	32	3	7	27	15

*Batted for Pfeister in eighth inning.
Errors—O'Leary, Rossman, Coughlin.

Detroit ....1 0 0 0 0 5 0 2 0—8
Chicago ....0 0 0 3 0 0 0 0 0—3

Two-base hits—Thomas, Cobb. Three-base hit —Hofman. Hits—Off Pfeister, 12 in 8 innings. Stolen bases—Evers, Chance, 2; Cobb, 2, Rossman, Steinfeldt. Double plays—Evers and Chance; Schaefer and Rossman; Hofman and Kling; O'Leary, Schaefer, and Rossman. Left on bases—Chicago, 3; Detroit, 6. First base on balls—Off Pfeister, 3; off Mullin, 1. First base on errors—Chicago, 2. Struck out—By Pfeister, 1; by Mullin, 8. Time of game—2:05. Umpires —Messrs. O'Day and Sheridan.

MINER BROWN STOPS DETROIT SLUGGERS

Chicago's Famous Pitcher Shuts Out the Tigers in World's Series Game.

THIRD VICTORY FOR CUBS

Detroit Must Win To-day to Still Have Chance of Capturing the Highest Honors in Baseball.

SCORING RUNDOWN

INNING THREE:
With a scoreless first and second inning the Cubs came through in the top of the third with two runs. Wildfire Schulte and Frank Chance scored on base hits by Harry Steinfeldt and Solly Hofman.
Cubs 2 Tigers 0

INNING NINE:
The game was quiet the rest of the way until the Cubs scored an unearned run in the top of the ninth on a Ty Cobb error on a ground ball by Frank Chance. Johnny Evers scored the run. The inning ended on an exciting play with Schulte called out trying to steal home. Frank Chance was on first base and broke for second giving Schulte the opportunity to break for home. Catcher Boss Schmidt threw the ball to second and Red Downs threw it right back to Schmidt who proceeded to tag out Schulte.
Cubs 3 Tigers 0

FINAL SCORE

Cubs 3 Tigers 0

Mordecai Brown pitched a complete game four hit shutout for the Cubs giving him his second win of the series, tying Overall. The two combined for the four Cubs wins in the series

THE BOX SCORE

CHICAGO.	AB	R	H	PO	A	DETROIT.	AB	R	H	PO	A
Sheck'd. rf.	4	0	0	0	0	M'Int're. lf.	4	0	0	1	0
Evers, 2b...	5	1	1	0	4	O'Leary, ss.	4	0	2	2	8
Schulte, rf.	8	1	2	0	0	Crawf'd. cf.	4	0	2	2	0
Chance. 1b.	4	1	8	17	0	Cobb. rf....	8	0	0	1	0
St'nf'dt. 8b.	8	0	1	2	8	R'sman, 1b.	8	0	0	12	1
Hofman, cf.	4	0	2	1	0	Sch'fer, 2b.	8	0	0	2	8
Tinker, ss..	4	0	0	2	7	Schmidt, c.	8	0	0	8	8
Kling, c....	4	0	2	5	1	C'ghlin, 8b.	2	0	0	1	4
Brown, p...	4	0	0	0	4	Summers,p.	2	0	0	0	2
						Winter, p..	0	0	0	0	0
Total...	85	8	11	27	19	*D. Jones...	1	0	0	0	0
						Total...29	0	4	27	15	

*Batted for Summers in the ninth inning.

Chicago ....0 0 2 0 0 0 0 0 1—8
Detroit ....0 0 0 0 0 0 0 0 0—0

Hits—Off Summers, 9 in eight innings; off Winter, 2 in one inning. Two-base hit—Crawford. Sacrifice hit—Steinfeldt. Stolen bases—Evers, Schulte, (2,) Hofman. Bases on balls—Off Summers, 8; off Winter, 1. Hit by pitcher —By Brown, 1. Left on bases—Detroit, 8; Chicago, 10. Struck out—By Summers, 5; by Brown, 4. Double play—Brown, Tinker, and Chance. Passed balls—Schmidt, Kling. Time of game—One hour and thirty-two minutes. Umpires—Messrs. Connolly and Klem.

CUBS SUPREME IN BASEBALL WORLD

Final Victory · Over Detroit Gives Chicago Team Greatest Record in History of the Game.

TIGERS ARE BEATEN, 2-0.

Overall Holds the Jungle Men to Three Hits, While the Little Bears Pound "Wild Bill" Donovan.

SCORING RUNDOWN

INNING ONE:
With one out Johnny Evers singled to center. Wildfire Schulte singled to left, advancing Evers to second. Frank Chance then drove him in with a single of his own.
Cubs 1 Tigers 0

Innings two, three and four were scoreless.

INNING FIVE:
Joe Tinker had a hit taken away from him when Tiger shortstop Charley O'Leary made a diving catch of a short blooper. Johnny Kling followed that with a walk and Orvie Overall bunted him to second before Jimmy Sheckard also walked. Runners were at first and second with two outs. Johnny Evers lined the first pitch to left center for a double, driving in Kling.
Cubs 2 Tigers 0

FINAL SCORE

Cubs 2 Tigers 0

THE BOX SCORE

CHICAGO.	AB	R	H	PO	A		DETROIT.	AB	R	H	PO	A
Sheck'd, lf.	3	0	1	2	0		M'Int're, lf.	3	0	1	2	0
Evers, 2b..	4	1	3	2	3		O'Leary, ss.	3	0	0	2	2
Schulte, rf.	3	0	1	0	0		Crawf'd, cf.	4	0	1	3	0
Chance, 1b.	4	0	3	10	0		Cobb, rf...	3	0	0	1	0
St'nf'dt, 3b.	2	0	0	0	3		R'sman, 1b.	4	0	0	7	3
Hofman, cf.	4	0	0	2	0		Sch'fer, 2b.	3	0	0	3	1
Tinker, ss..	4	0	1	1	4		Schmidt, c.	4	0	0	5	4
Kling ,c...	3	1	0	10	2		C'ghlin, 3b.	3	0	1	2	1
Overall, p..	2	0	1	0	0		Donovan, p.	2	0	0	1	1
Total...	29	2	10	27	12		Total...	29	0	3*26	12	

&Overall out, hit by Sheckard's batted ball.

Detroit	0	0	0	0	0	0	0	0	0—0
Chicago	1	0	0	0	1	0	0	0	0—2

Two-base hits—McIntyre, Evers. Sacrifice hits—Schulte, Steinfeldt, Overall. Stolen base —Donovan. First base on balls—Off Donovan, 3; off Overall, 4. Left on bases—Detroit, 7; Chicago, 6. Struck out—By Donovan, 3; by Overall, 10. Double plays—Schmidt, Schaefer, and Schmidt; O'Leary, Rossman, and Coughlin. Wild pitch—Overall. Time of game—One hour and twenty-four minutes. Umpires— Messrs. Sheridan and O'Day.

IN CONCLUSION

The Cubs in 1908 were the world champions. That can never be taken away from them. What can happen is people forgetting about them and that's something I hope this book helps prevent. Although the sport has changed considerably since then, it's people such as these who built the foundation on which the sport stands today. Because this book is about the Cubs it can and should be considered a regional story but in reality it's about something more. It's a reminder of other times, teams and players making up baseball's early days.

Chicago fought a close battle that year with the Giants and Pirates to win the National League championship before winning the World Series somewhat handily. Two years earlier they won the National League crown handily, winning 116 games, but then lost the series to the White Sox, who get and deserve credit for being world champions. Does that mean the World Series is more important? Of course not because it's the season-long battle that gets teams there and gives them the right to fight for the championship. That battle is the reason the other teams should be remembered also.

As most people know things haven't been easy for the Cubs since 1908. While they appeared in the World Series six times since then they haven't emerged successful. 1910, 1918, 1929, 1932, 1938 and 1945 were their other World Series appearances in the 20th century. They won a total of seven games in all those Series combined. There have been some memorable moments and players though. Playoff and World

Series near-misses, no hitters, MVP's, Cy Young awards and batting championships to name some of those moments. No matter what the team has been doing there has always been someone or something to root for.

Those moments and players provide more reasons why it's important to remember the past.

For Cub fans, every year is 'next year'. Until they win the championship again, which they surely will one day, let's never forget the past or not allow the past be explained to us, which this book is meant to do. You don't need to have been alive to know about those times. In the case of the Cubs many generations have come and gone and there are few if any people left who could remember that far in the past.

Until they one day do win the championship maybe we can think about Frank Chance leading the charge in the very early 1900's. About Joe Tinker and Johnny Evers combining for the first out of a double play before Chance catches the ball at first for out number two. For the third out of the inning maybe we can imagine Johnny Kling throwing out a runner at second on a steal attempt, helping Orvie Overall out of a jam.

Think about Three Fingers Brown throwing another impressive complete game with his famous curve ball for one of his many wins in the season. It can be fun to imagine.

Until they win again, let's keep waiting for next year as we always have done.

1908 TEAM STATISTICS

OFFENSE

PLAYER	G	AB	HR	HBP	SB	AVG
Johnny Evers	126	416	0	5	36	.300
Johnny Kling	126	424	4	3	16	.276
Frank Chance	129	452	2	8	27	.272
Joe Tinker	157	548	6	0	30	.266
Harry Steinfeldt	150	539	1	4	12	.241
Frank Shulte	102	386	1	3	15	.236
Jimmy Sheckard	115	403	2	2	18	.231
Jimmy Slagle	104	352	0	0	17	.222
Doc Marshall	12	20	0	0	0	.300
Heinie Zimmerman	46	113	0	0	2	.292
Del Howard	96	315	1	5	11	.279
Pat Moran	50	150	0	1	6	.260
Kid Durbin	14	28	0	1	0	.250
Solly Hofman	120	411	2	6	15	.243
Jack Hayden	11	45	0	0	1	.200
Vin Campbell	1	1	0	0	0	.000

DEFENSE

PLAYER	GAMES	ASSISTS	ERRORS
Frank Shulte	102	8	1
Jimmy Slagle	101	6	5
Jimmy Sheckard	115	13	10
Frank Chance	126	86	15
Johnny Kling	117	153	16
Johnny Evers	122	361	25
Harry Steinfeldt	150	275	28
Joe Tinker	157	570	39
Kid Durbin	14	0	0
Jack Hayden	11	0	0
Doc Marshall	7	4	1
Del Howard	86	12	6
Heinie Zimmerman	30	48	9
Pat Moran	45	56	10
Solly Hofman	118	97	23

PITCHING

PLAYER	G	W	L	ERA	S
Mordecai Brown	44	29	9	1.47	5
Ed Reulbach	46	24	7	2.03	1
Orval Overall	37	15	11	1.92	4
Jack Pfeister	22	12	10	2.00	0
Chick Fraser	26	11	9	2.27	2
Carl Lundgren	23	6	9	4.22	0
Andy Coakley	4	2	0	0.89	0
Rube Kroh	2	0	0	1.50	0
Carl Spongberg	1	0	0	9.00	0
Bill Mack	2	0	0	3.00	0

1908 EVENTS

- Oil discovered in Iran.
- Boy Scouts started.
- Dr. Jekyll & Mr. Hyde movie premieres in Chicago.
- Enckes comet hits Siberia.
- Sacrifice fly adopted, repealed in 1931 and adopted again in 1954.
- Cincinnati mayor Mark Breith announces that "women are not physically fit to operate automobiles".
- The Mills Committee declares that baseball was invented by Abner Doubleday.
- Groundbreaking begins on Philadelphia's Shibe Park where the Phillies played until 1970. It was torn down in 1976.
- Mother's Day was observed for the first time.
- The first passenger flight in an airplane took place on May 14th.
- Orville Wright makes the first one hour plane flight.
- General Motors was incorporated.
- The Ford Model T goes on the market for $825. It was sold in black only.
- William Howard Taft is elected 27th president.
- Jack Johnson becomes the first black heavyweight champion.
- New York City passes a law banning women from smoking in public.
- Katie Mulcahey is the first woman to break the no smoking law.
- The New York to Paris automobile race took place with George Schuster winning after an eighty eight day ride.
- A subway connecting Brooklyn and Manhattan opens.

- Theodore Roosevelt proclaims the Grand Canyon a National Monument, later to become a National Park.
- "Take Me Out To The Ballgame" is written by Jack Norworth.
- The Wright Brothers get a patent for their airplane.
- The Lusitania crosses the Atlantic Ocean in record time.

1908 BIRTHS

- Milton Berle 1908 – 2002

- Bette Davis 1908 – 1989

- Alistair Cooke 1908 – 2004

- Jimmy Stewart 1908 – 1997

- Edward R. Murrow 1908 – 1965

- Lyndon B. Johnson 1908 – 1973

- Red Barber 1908 – 1992

- Joan Crawford 1908 – 1997

- Buddy Ebsen 1908 – 2003

- Ian Fleming 1908 – 1964

- Mel Blanc 1908 – 1989

- Nelson Rockefeller 1908 – 1979

- Carol Lombard 1908 – 1942

- Barry Goldwater 1908 – 1998

1908 DEATHS

- Geronimo - renowned Apache chief and military leader. Of pneumonia.

- Grover Cleveland – 22nd and 24th president. Of a heart attack.

- Butch Cassidy, outlaw and co-founder of the Hole In The Wall Gang. Gunned down in Buenos Aires, Argentina.

- The Sundance Kid, born Harry Alonzo Longabaugh. Outlaw and co-founder of the Hole In The Wall Gang Gunned down in Buenos Aires, Argentina.

- Nikolai Rimsky Korsakov – Russian composer known for 'The Flight Of The Bumblebee' and 'Scheherazade'. Of debilitating angina.

- First Lieutenant Thomas Selfridge – killed when he was a passenger in a plane flown by Orville Wright when it crashed in Fort Meyers, Florida.

- Between 80,000 and 200,000 die in an earthquake and resulting tsunami in Messina Straits, Italy.

- 180 die in a Collingwood, Ohio primary school fire.

- Between 130 and 160 die in a mine explosion in Marianna, Pennsylvania.

Baseball's Sad Lexicon

These are the saddest of possible words:
"Tinker to Evers to Chance."
Trio of bear cubs, and fleeter than birds,
Tinker and Evers and Chance.
Ruthlessly pricking our gonfalon bubble,
Making a Giant hit into a double - -
Words that are heavy with nothing but trouble:
"Tinker to Evers to Chance."

Written by Franklin Pierce Adams in 1910.

Franklin Pierce Adams was a newspaper columnist for the New York Evening Mail when he wrote this poem on July 10, 1910. He was traveling to the Polo Grounds to see a game between the Cubs and Giants when he wrote it.

He was born and raised in Chicago and was initially a Cub fan. His first newspaper job was in Chicago with the Chicago Journal in 1903 at the age of twenty one before moving on to the New York Evening Mail the next year, working there until 1913. His baseball loyalty turned to the New York Giants as he spent many years in New York cheering them on.

A dictionary definition of a gonfalon is 'a banner suspended from a crossbar'. In this case that would be a pennant which signifies the championship so what he means when he says they are 'pricking our gonfalon bubble' is that they are ruining the Giants chances of winning a championship. Bursting their bubble.

The phrase 'making a Giant hit into a double' can be misleading also. He is not referring to a double as a base hit double but rather as a double play. They are taking away what would be hits and turning them into double plays.

Cub third baseman Harry Steinfeldt is the only Cub infielder not included in the poem which is a small claim to fame that he was occasionally reminded of.

Because of the notoriety of the poem there were more verses added occasionally by other writers but the original poem consists of those eight lines.

Joe Tinker, Johnny Evers and Frank Chance were a double play combination that began in late 1902 and lasted until April of 1912.

Franklin Pierce Adams remained a newspaper columnist until 1941 and worked in radio until 1948. He died on March 23, 1960 at seventy eight years of age. It has been said that he suffered from Alzheimer's late in his life.

He did write and publish other poems, mostly of the humorous variety but Baseball's Sad Lexicon is by far his most famous.

Made in the USA